Machines Inside Machines

Using Wheels and Axles

Wendy Sadler

Raintree

www.raintreepublishers.co.uk
Visit our website to find out more information about **Raintree** books.

To order:
☎ Phone 44 (0) 1865 888113
▤ Send a fax to 44 (0) 1865 314091
▭ Visit the Raintree Bookshop at **www.raintreepublishers.co.uk** to browse our catalogue and order online.

First published in Great Britain by Raintree, Halley Court, Jordan Hill, Oxford OX2 8EJ, part of Harcourt Education.
Raintree is a registered trademark of Harcourt Education Ltd.

Editorial: Melanie Copland and Kate Buckingham
Design: Michelle Lisseter, Victoria Bevan and Bridge Creative Services Ltd
Picture Research: Hannah Taylor
Production: Duncan Gilbert

Originated by Repro Multi Warna
Printed and bound in China by South China Printing Company

ISBN 1 844 43606 3 (hardback)
09 08 07 06 05
10 9 8 7 6 5 4 3 2 1

British Library Cataloguing in Publication Data
Sadler, Wendy
Using Wheels and Axles. – (Machines Inside Machines)
621.8'11
A full catalogue record for this book is available from the British Library.

Acknowledgements
The publishers would like to thank the following for permission to reproduce photographs:
Alamy Images (David Wall) p. **4**; Alamy Images (Motoring Picture Library) p. **16**; Corbis (Mark Cooper) p. **22**; Corbis (Paul A. Souders) p. **11**; Corbis (Paul Barton) p. **19**; Corbis (Pawel Libera) p. **29**; Corbis (The Purcell Team) p. **24**; Getty Images (Photodisc) p. **6**; Getty Images (Stone) p. **26**; Harcourt Education Ltd (Peter Morris) p. **9**; Harcourt Education Ltd (Tudor Photography) pp. **5, 7, 8, 10, 12, 13, 14, 15, 17, 18, 20, 23, 25, 27**; Robert Adams "How to design & make Automata" p. **21**; Science Photo Library (Biomedical Imaging Unit, Southampton General Hospital) p. **28**.

Cover photograph of a wheel reproduced with permission of Powerstock/ age fotostock.

Every effort has been made to contact copyright holders of any material reproduced in this book. Any omissions will be rectified in subsequent printings if notice is given to the publishers.

The paper used to print this book comes from sustainable resources.

Contents

Any words appearing in the text in bold, **like this,** are explained in the glossary.

Machines with wheels and axles

Wheels are all around us! Just think of how many times you see a wheel every day. A wheel does not work by itself. It always needs an **axle**. Have you ever seen one of those?

A wheel and axle together make a type of **simple machine**. A simple machine is a **tool** that makes a job easier to do.

Without the wheel and axle we would not be able to travel on cars and trains.

Wheels and axles are not just used on vehicles. All sorts of different machines use them for many different types of job. Wheels and axles are simple machines that can turn **linear motion** into **rotary motion**. Linear motion is movement forwards and backwards. Rotary motion is movement round and round.

Clocks use wheels and axles to help us tell the time. Can you see the wheels and axles in the back of this alarm clock?

What is a wheel?

Wheels were **invented** thousands of years ago. When people wanted to move things around they used logs as **rollers** to make the job easier. They put heavy objects on top of the logs and rolled them along the ground. Having these rollers meant there was less **friction** between the objects and the ground. When two surfaces rub together we get friction which is a **force**. It can slow things down or stop them moving.

Rollers are still used today to move heavy objects.

690-820-0030

What would happen without...?

Imagine trying to go skateboarding without wheels. The board would hardly move when you pushed off because of the friction between the board and the ground!

Activity

1. Try sliding a book across a tabletop with one push. How far did it go?
2. Now rest the book on a few pencils or pens and try again. How far did it go this time?

   The book should move further when you push it on top of the pencils. The pencils are acting like rollers. Rollers help us to move things using less **effort force**. This is the force that has to be put into something to make it work. In this activity, the effort force came from your hand pushing the book.

effort force

What is an axle?

A wheel or **roller** is more useful when it is used with an **axle**. Some axles are fixed to the object that is moving. A fixed axle just lets the wheel spin around without the axle moving as well. The front wheel of a bicycle has this kind of axle. When you turn the wheel it moves around, but the axle does not turn. If you fix a wheel and axle together they become a **simple machine**.

wheel

axle

Activity

1. Have a look at the back wheel on a bicycle.
2. Turn the pedals. Which part of the wheel is the pedal joined to? The outside wheel is larger than the axle in the middle. When you turn the axle a small distance, the outside of the wheel moves a larger distance.

A doorknob is a type of wheel and axle. The part that you hold is the large wheel. Hidden inside the doorknob is a rod that goes through the door. This is the axle. The **effort force** used to turn the doorknob is made into a bigger **resulting force**. The resulting force is the force that comes out of a simple machine. In this example, the resulting force turns the axle. The axle pulls the door catch in, so the door can open.

wheel

A doorknob is a type of wheel and axle.

How do wheels and axles help us?

There are two main ways that wheels and **axles** can help us. In doorknobs and taps we use wheels and axles to turn a small **force** into a larger force. You do not use much force to turn the head of a tap, but you do turn it a long way. The axle in the middle of the tap does not travel so far because it is smaller. This means that there is more force pushing the axle which turns the tap on.

wheel

axle

This garden tap uses a wheel and axle.

The Penny Farthing bicycle has a large front wheel and needs lots of effort to make it go!

large wheel

pedal

Another thing that wheels and axles can do is to turn a small distance into a larger distance. An old bicycle called a Penny Farthing used this idea. A Penny Farthing has a very large front wheel, and a small back wheel. By turning the pedals a small distance you can make the large wheel move a lot. The distance that the bicycle moves is much more than the distance your feet move.

Wheels and axles for transport

Inside some wheels there are **bearings** that let the wheel turn smoothly around the **axle**. These bearings are usually small metal balls that can move in all directions. In some machines where the axle is fixed to the wheel, an **engine** turns the axle. The axle then turns the wheel and the machine moves.

In machines where the wheel turns freely around the axle, something else must make the machine move.

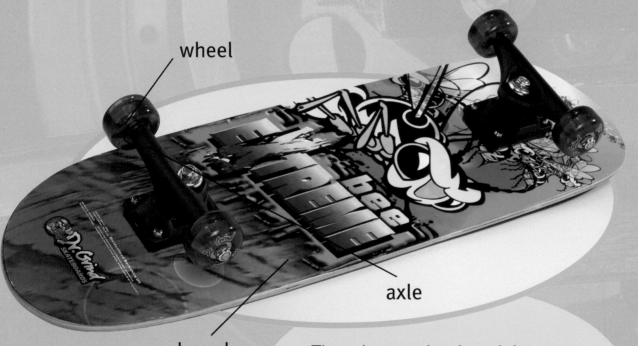

wheel

axle

board

The axle on a skateboard does not turn the wheels. It is fixed to the board, so the wheels move freely when you push off with your foot.

Wheels on bicycles and cars have **tyres** on them. These are made of rubber. Tyres help in two ways. The rubber helps the bicycle or car to **grip** the road. The tyre is also full of air. The air in tyres cushions you from the bumps in the road. Train wheels do not need tyres because they travel on smooth metal train tracks, which do not feel bumpy.

What would happen without...?

Have you ever ridden a bicycle with a flat tyre? What was it like? Without tyres, bicycle journeys would be very uncomfortable!

Wheels and axles around the house

Would you guess that a screwdriver is a type of wheel and **axle**? In a screwdriver the wheel and axle are fixed and turn together. The handle of the screwdriver is the wheel and the rod or metal part is the axle. A screwdriver is used to make the turning **force** of your hand bigger.

Activity

1. Ask an adult for two different size screwdrivers and a soft tape measure.
2. Measure around the widest part of each screwdriver.
3. Measure around the metal rods that turn screws.

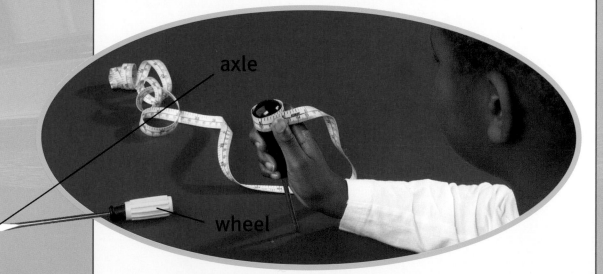

axle

wheel

The screwdriver that has the biggest difference between the handle and the rod is the one that can be used to undo really tight screws. A wider head means you are turning a long distance into a big force.

When you press "play" on your CD player an axle turns the CD.

wheel

hole for axle

A CD player has
a wheel and axle.
The axle goes through the hole in the
CD to keep it in place. The CD turns with the axle.
The axle is turned at a fast speed, but travels a small
distance. The CD – which is the wheel – moves a larger
distance at the same time.

Unexpected wheels and axles!

Wheels and **axles** are found all over the place. These are all types of wheels and axles that you might find in a car:

- ◗ steering wheel
- ◗ dial to tune the radio or turn up the volume
- ◗ window winder.

What would happen without...?

Without a steering wheel and axle the driver would have to get out and move the car wheels in the right direction at every corner. This would be very hard work and make journeys take a long time!

Can you imagine how long it would take to drive along a winding road without a steering wheel?

A pizza cutter uses a wheel and axle. Can you see any other wheels and axles in your kitchen?

In the kitchen there are lots of different types of wheels and axles. A pizza cutter uses a wheel to change the direction of the **effort force** you put in. You push down with the handle and the wheel turns round to move the blade through the pizza. The blade changes the pushing down **force** into a force that pushes the pizza slices apart.

Part of the lever family

The wheel and **axle** are part of the **lever** family of machines. A lever is a long stick that turns around a point called a **fulcrum** (or pivot). Imagine a bicycle wheel that has lots of spokes. Each of these spokes is like a little lever. Each little lever moves in a circle around the fulcrum. The fulcrum of these levers is the axle in the centre of the wheel.

wheel

spoke

axle

Each spoke of the bicycle wheel is a lever that turns around the axle.

A fishing rod uses lots of **simple machines** together. The handle on the **reel** is a lever that turns a wheel. The reel is the axle. When you catch a fish you need a big **force** to pull it in. You use the handle to turn the wheel. The **effort force** you use to turn the handle is changed into a larger force on the reel. You have to turn the handle many times to make enough force to bring the fish in, but you do not need to use much force.

reel (axle)

Fishing rods use a wheel and axle to bring fish in once they have been hooked.

handle (lever)

19

shaped wheels

A cam is a type of wheel and **axle** that can be used to change the direction of movement. A cam can be egg shaped, or it can be made so that the axle is not in the middle of the wheel. A cam can be used to turn **rotary motion** into **vertical motion**.

Activity

1. Ask an adult to help you.
2. Cut out an egg shape from some thick paper or card.
3. Carefully make a hole somewhere in the egg shape by pushing a pencil through it.
4. Rest some paper on top of the egg shape.
5. Slowly spin the pencil round and watch how the paper moves up and down.

Cams can be used to make toy models of people and animals move. Different shaped cams are joined to one long axle. When you turn the axle the models resting on the cams move up and down.

lever
(joined to axle)

When you turn the axle on this machine the cams go round and round but the models move up and down.

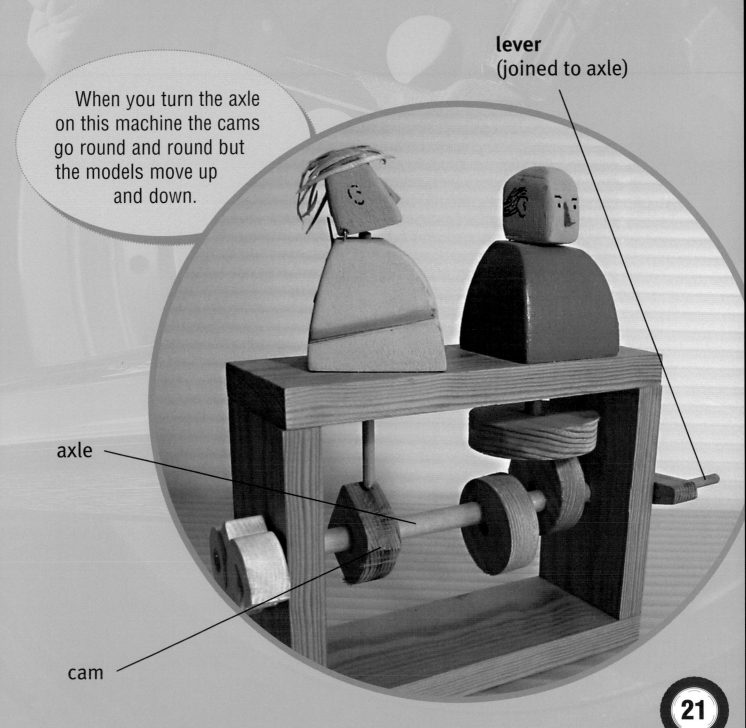

axle

cam

Wheels with teeth

Wheels with teeth around the edges are called **cogs**. A cog cannot work by itself – it must work with another cog to be useful. Cogs turn around on an **axle**. The teeth of one cog fit into the spaces between the teeth of another cog.

Using lots of cogs together you can turn one wheel and make another wheel move, even if it is far away.

Cogs are usually used to change the direction or speed of movement.

Two cogs used together will change the direction of movement. When you turn the first cog, the teeth push against the teeth in the second cog. This push makes the second cog move in the opposite direction.

If you have two cogs of different sizes you can change the speed of the movement. Turning a small cog quickly will make a larger cog turn, but it will turn more slowly. Different-sized cogs working together are called **gears**.

Have you ever looked at the gears on the wheel of a bicycle? Can you see the cogs?

Ropes and belts

wheel

axle

If you wrap a rope around a wheel and **axle** you can make a pulley. A pulley is used to help lift heavy things. If the rope goes around lots of wheels, the pulley can lift very heavy objects.

If a pulley has a rope wrapped around four wheels you have to pull the rope four times as far, but you only need to use one quarter of the **force**. That makes it much easier!

This pulley is being used to lift a bucket of water out of a well.

A yo-yo is a wheel and axle with a string wrapped around the axle. When you let go of the yo-yo it falls because of gravity. Gravity is a force that pulls everything down towards the ground. As the yo-yo falls down, the string unwinds from the axle. This makes the yo-yo spin. When all of the string has unwound, you can tug on the string to make the yo-yo spin back up again.

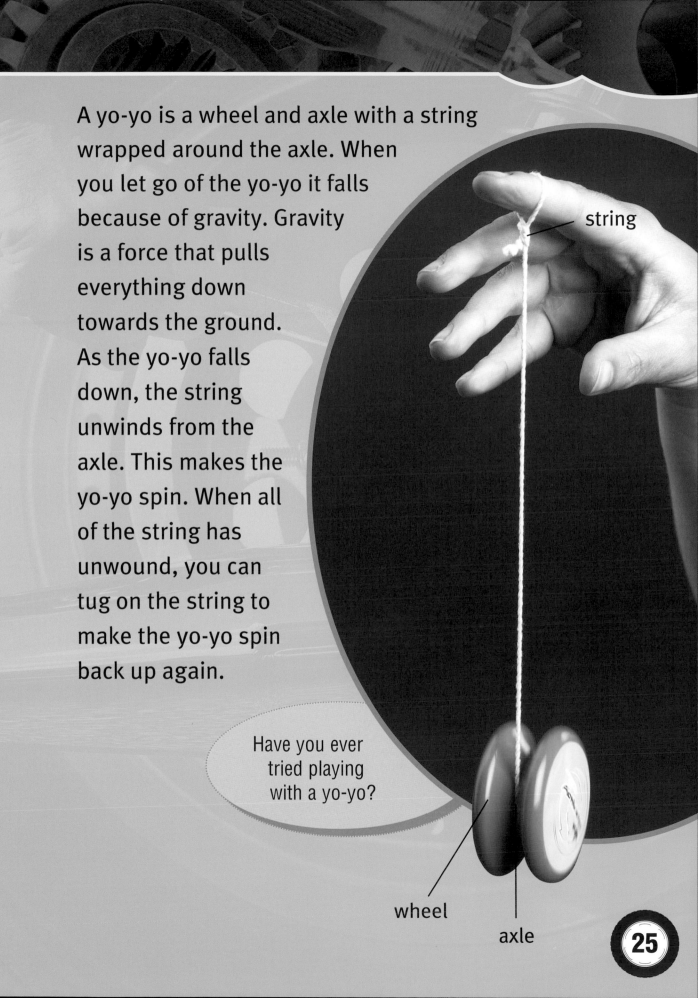

string

Have you ever tried playing with a yo-yo?

wheel

axle

Playful wheels and axles

A roundabout in a playground is a large wheel and **axle**. The axle is where the roundabout is joined to the ground. The wheel is the place where you stand. You can make the roundabout turn quite easily by pushing it at the edge of the wheel. You need less **force** than if you were trying to turn it from near the middle, but you need to travel a larger distance.

To turn a roundabout you need to push it from the edge.

wheel

axle

A spinning top is also a type of wheel and axle. Inside the top there is another **simple machine**, a screw. When you push down on the handle the screw moves down. This makes the axle in the middle turn. The axle is joined to the rest of the spinning top, so the top turns as well.

Have you ever played with a spinning top?

From tiny to huge...

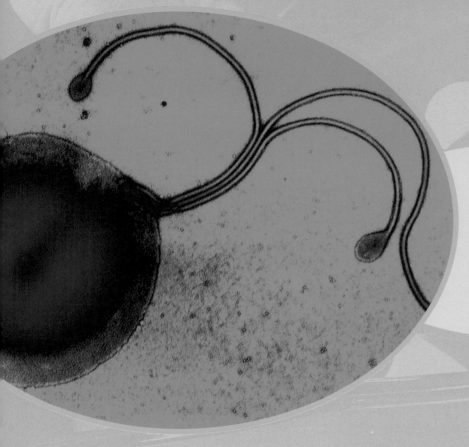

This tiny creature is a bacterium. It swims around using the smallest wheel and axle we know about.

The smallest wheels on Earth are found in some tiny creatures called bacteria. Bacteria are very simple animals that live in soil, water, or inside other plants and animals. Some types of bacteria move around by spinning a long tail called a flagella. This tail moves around the main body of the bacteria which acts like a simple wheel and **axle**. As it spins it pushes the bacteria along.

The largest wheels on Earth can be found in fairgrounds. Ferris wheels are huge wheels that you can ride on. The wheel is driven by an **engine**, which makes the axle turn. The large wheel with seats on is joined to the axle. When the axle is turned, the large wheel moves as well. One of the biggest wheels in the world is called the London Eye.

The London Eye is a wheel that is about as tall as fifteen houses!

Find out for yourself

You can find out about **simple machines** by talking to your teacher or parents. Think about the simple machines you use every day – how do you think they work? Your local library will have books and information about this. You will find the answers to many of your questions in this book, but you can also use other books and the Internet.

Books to read

Science Around Us: Using Machines, Sally Hewitt (Chrysalis Children's Books, 2004)

Very Useful Machines: Wheels, Chris Oxlade (Heinemann Library, 2003)

What do Wheels and Cranks do? David Glover (Heinemann Library, 2002)

Using the Internet

Explore the Internet to find out more about wheels and **axles**. Try using a search engine such as www.yahooligans.com or www.internet4kids.com , and type in keywords such as 'wheel', 'axle', and **'tyres'**.

Glossary

axle rod that goes through the centre of a wheel or group of wheels

bearings small balls, usually made of metal, that can help a wheel to turn smoothly

cog wheel with teeth around the edge

effort force force that you put into a wheel and axle

engine machine that can make things move

force push or pull. Forces can make things move.

friction something that happens when two surfaces rub against each other. Friction can slow things down or stop them moving.

fulcrum fixed part of a lever that the bar or stick moves around

gears wheels with teeth (cogs) working together to change the direction or speed of movement

grip hold on to

invent to discover or make something for the first time

lever stiff bar or stick that moves around a fixed point called a fulcrum

linear motion backwards and forwards movement

reel part of a fishing rod that the line is wrapped around

resulting force push or pull that you get out of a wheel and axle

rollers rounded rods that objects can be put on to roll them along

rotary motion round and round movement

simple machine something that can change the effort force needed to move something, or change the direction it moves in

tool something that helps us to do a certain job

tyre rubber covering around a wheel

vertical motion upwards and downwards movement

Index